Quick Revision

KS1: Age 5–6

Mental Maths

Hilary Koll and Steve Mills

First published 2007
exclusively for WHSmith by
Hodder Education, part of Hachette Livre UK,
338 Euston Road, London NW1 3BH

Impression number   10 9 8 7 6 5 4 3 2
Year   2010 2009 2008

Text and illustrations © Hodder Education 2007

Text: Hilary Koll and Steve Mills
Cover illustration: Sally Newton Illustrations

Typeset by Fakenham Photosetting Limited, Fakenham, Norfolk

ISBN 978 0 340 94980 1

Printed and bound in the UK by Hobbs the Printers.

For parents

WHSmith Mental Maths

- Mental maths is an essential part of children's mathematics. It enables children to deal with numerical situations quickly and confidently. It is a central part of the National Curriculum and National Primary Strategy and is tested as part of the National and Optional Tests throughout children's primary education.
- Mental maths is underpinned by a knowledge of number facts that can be quickly recalled, without the need to 'work them out'. These number facts include knowing doubles of numbers, addition and subtraction facts for small numbers, multiplication tables facts and the related division facts.
- This book provides opportunity for testing children's knowledge of these facts and their abilities to use them to find other answers quickly. Regular practice of these skills helps children to build this good mathematical foundation and to gain confidence in all other numeracy work.

How this book can help your child

This book contains practice of the essential areas expected of children aged 5–6, including testing their abilities to solve word problems. This is a skill that is tested at school throughout the primary age range. Children of this age are expected to master the following number facts and mental strategies:

- Derive and recall all pairs of numbers with a total of 10 and addition facts for totals to at least 5; work out the corresponding subtraction facts
- Count on or back in ones, twos, fives and tens and use this knowledge to derive the multiples of 2, 5 and 10 to the tenth multiple
- Recall the doubles of all numbers to at least 10
- Solve problems involving counting, adding, subtracting and doubling in the context of numbers, measures or money.

How you can help your child

Below are some suggestions for ways in which you can help your child to memorise number facts and to use them to derive new facts.

Help children to enjoy learning the facts – everyone learns best when they are enjoying themselves! Give rewards for when facts are learnt and praise your child for any progress made when working through this book.

- Have a fact for the day! If a child is struggling with memorising a fact, such as $8 - 3 = 5$, and is unable to say the answer without working it out make it the fact of the day.
  Ask your child, as he or she goes about everyday life to repeat the fact in different ways, e.g. *whisper it, shout it, say it in a croaky voice, in a squeaky voice, in different accents, as you are jumping down the stairs, in the car,* and so on. Encourage your child to say the fact using a range of different maths words, e.g. for addition use the words add, and, plus, makes, equals; and for subtraction use take away, minus, subtract, etc. Keep a list of the facts of the day and come back to them at the end of the week.
- Swap facts around. Talk to your child about how learning one fact actually means that many facts are learnt, e.g. if you know that $3 + 5 = 8$, then you know that $5 + 3 = 8$ and that $8 - 3 = 5$ and $8 - 5 = 3$. Say the fact of the day and ask your child to say which other facts this helps them to learn.
- Show facts on number lines to help children build up a picture of where numbers are in relation to one another.

For 5 + 3

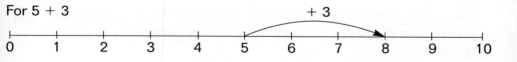

For 9 − 4

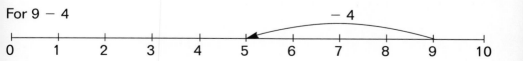

For 4 lots of 2 or 4 × 2

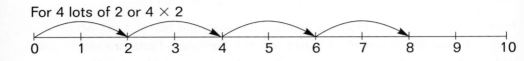

For 'How many 2s in 6?' or 6 ÷ 2

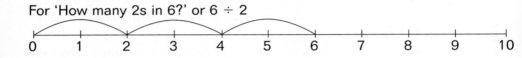

- Make flashcards. On an old envelope, piece of paper or card write the facts that your child is finding difficult to learn. Write the answers on the back and encourage your child to test themselves and check by turning over the card.
- Point out patterns in the number facts, such as that all the answers to the two, four, six, eight and ten times tables are even numbers, e.g. 2 × 7 = 14, 3 × 10 = 30, 4 × 8 = 32.
- Show your child how doubles can be used to help learn other facts, e.g. if you know that double 6 is 12, then 6 + 7 is one more than double 6 and so is 13.
- Ask questions about real-life situations to help practise these skills, e.g. when counting out knives or forks for a meal ask questions such as 'There are ten knives in the drawer and I take out 4, how many are left?' or 'We need 6 forks. I have 2 here, how many more do I need?'. These situations encourage children to realise the importance of learning number facts and give them vital opportunities to practise these skills.

How to use this book

To get the most from this book

- Encourage your child to take the tests regularly, ideally one per day.
- Repetition of facts is important if children are to memorise and learn to recall them effectively. The more often a child practises their number facts the more likely they are to retain them over a longer period. Some tests contain the same question more than once for this reason.
- Read the first question aloud in different ways, e.g. use the words 'add', 'plus', etc. to help your child recognise what to do, e.g. whether to add, double or take away.
- Time each test. As your child becomes more confident, the time should decrease.
- If the early tests take more than 15 minutes to complete, suggest that your child tackles each row one at a time with a break in-between.
- Involve your child in marking the tests and talk together about any incorrect answers. Be sensitive and draw more attention to those that were correct, asking your child to tell you whether they had to work out the answer or whether they know the fact 'off by heart'. Agree to make a fact that your child found difficult the new 'fact for the day' to practise.
- Write the times and marks on the record sheet on page 6.
- Draw attention to improvements made in the times or marks.
- Praise and encourage your child at all stages.

Mental Maths record sheet

Test 1	Mark	/40	Time taken	
Test 2	Mark	/40	Time taken	
Test 3	Mark	/40	Time taken	
Test 4	Mark	/40	Time taken	
Test 5	Mark	/40	Time taken	
Test 6	Mark	/40	Time taken	
Test 7	Mark	/40	Time taken	
Test 8	Mark	/40	Time taken	
Test 9	Mark	/40	Time taken	
Test 10	Mark	/40	Time taken	
Test 11	Mark	/40	Time taken	
Test 12	Mark	/10	Time taken	
Test 13	Mark	/40	Time taken	
Test 14	Mark	/40	Time taken	
Test 15	Mark	/30	Time taken	
Test 16	Mark	/30	Time taken	
Test 17	Mark	/40	Time taken	
Test 18	Mark	/40	Time taken	
Test 19	Mark	/40	Time taken	
Test 20	Mark	/40	Time taken	
Test 21	Mark	/10	Time taken	

Test 1

Addition facts of totals to 5

a   3 + 2 =   2 + 3 =   3 + 1 =   1 + 1 =

b   2 + 1 =   2 + 4 =   0 + 4 =   0 + 2 =

c   1 + 3 =   4 + 4 =   2 + 2 =   3 + 0 =

d   3 + 1 =   3 + 0 =   1 + 3 =   4 + 1 =

e   3 + 3 =   4 + 2 =   4 + 4 =   2 + 3 =

f   5 + 0 =   1 + 4 =   2 + 4 =   3 + 0 =

g   2 + 4 =   3 + 1 =   5 + 0 =   4 + 4 =

h   1 + 4 =   3 + 2 =   3 + 1 =   4 + 3 =

i   1 + 3 =   2 + 2 =   2 + 3 =   1 + 3 =

j   2 + 2 =   4 + 0 =   1 + 2 =   1 + 5 =

Mark   Time Taken

7

Test 2

Addition facts of totals to 5

a 4 + 1 =   5 + 2 =   1 + 3 =   1 + 2 =

b 2 + 3 =   4 + 3 =   2 + 1 =   1 + 3 =

c 5 + 0 =   4 + 1 =   1 + 4 =   4 + 0 =

d 5 + 2 =   1 + 2 =   4 + 0 =   2 + 3 =

e 3 + 1 =   2 + 2 =   4 + 1 =   5 + 1 =

f 3 + 3 =   5 + 1 =   2 + 0 =   2 + 1 =

g 2 + 4 =   3 + 1 =   3 + 3 =   3 + 0 =

h 3 + 3 =   5 + 3 =   4 + 2 =   2 + 4 =

i 2 + 2 =   5 + 0 =   5 + 3 =   3 + 3 =

j 4 + 2 =   1 + 2 =   1 + 4 =   4 + 4 =

Mark   Time Taken

8

Test 3

Addition of numbers with a total of 10

a 9 + ☐ = 10   10 + ☐ = 10   5 + ☐ = 10   3 + ☐ = 10

b 7 + ☐ = 10   6 + ☐ = 10   2 + ☐ = 10   5 + ☐ = 10

c 8 + ☐ = 10   1 + ☐ = 10   9 + ☐ = 10   4 + ☐ = 10

d 10 + ☐ = 10   7 + ☐ = 10   3 + ☐ = 10   6 + ☐ = 10

e 1 + ☐ = 10   4 + ☐ = 10   10 + ☐ = 10   7 + ☐ = 10

f ☐ + 9 = 10   ☐ + 10 = 10   ☐ + 3 = 10   ☐ + 2 = 10

g ☐ + 8 = 10   ☐ + 2 = 10   ☐ + 9 = 10   ☐ + 4 = 10

h ☐ + 1 = 10   ☐ + 5 = 10   ☐ + 2 = 10   ☐ + 8 = 10

i ☐ + 6 = 10   ☐ + 9 = 10   ☐ + 8 = 10   ☐ + 3 = 10

j ☐ + 1 = 10   ☐ + 8 = 10   ☐ + 4 = 10   ☐ + 5 = 10

Mark ☐   Time Taken ☐

9

Addition of numbers with a total of 10

a   10 + ☐ = 10   3 + ☐ = 10   9 + ☐ = 10   7 + ☐ = 10

b   9 + ☐ = 10   2 + ☐ = 10   3 + ☐ = 10   8 + ☐ = 10

c   3 + ☐ = 10   4 + ☐ = 10   6 + ☐ = 10   2 + ☐ = 10

d   6 + ☐ = 10   10 + ☐ = 10   8 + ☐ = 10   1 + ☐ = 10

e   2 + ☐ = 10   6 + ☐ = 10   4 + ☐ = 10   5 + ☐ = 10

f   ☐ + 6 = 10   ☐ + 5 = 10   ☐ + 3 = 10   ☐ + 2 = 10

g   ☐ + 8 = 10   ☐ + 0 = 10   ☐ + 6 = 10   ☐ + 9 = 10

h   ☐ + 10 = 10   ☐ + 9 = 10   ☐ + 4 = 10   ☐ + 0 = 10

i   ☐ + 5 = 10   ☐ + 10 = 10   ☐ + 7 = 10   ☐ + 3 = 10

j   ☐ + 2 = 10   ☐ + 4 = 10   ☐ + 9 = 10   ☐ + 1 = 10

Mark ☐   Time Taken ☐

Subtraction facts of numbers to 5

a   2 – 2 =   2 – 1 =   1 – 0 =   5 – 2 =

b   3 – 2 =   4 – 3 =   3 – 1 =   5 – 3 =

c   4 – 0 =   5 – 0 =   1 – 1 =   3 – 3 =

d   4 – 1 =   2 – 0 =   5 – 3 =   2 – 1 =

e   3 – 3 =   3 – 1 =   5 – 1 =   4 – 2 =

f   3 – 1 =   3 – 2 =   4 – 0 =   4 – 1 =

g   5 – 2 =   4 – 2 =   4 – 3 =   5 – 3 =

h   5 – 1 =   2 – 1 =   3 – 3 =   5 – 4 =

i   3 – 0 =   5 – 4 =   4 – 4 =   3 – 2 =

j   5 – 2 =   5 – 3 =   4 – 2 =   1 – 0 =

Mark   Time Taken

Test 6

Subtraction facts of numbers to 5

a 4 − 1 =   2 − 1 =   2 − 0 =   3 − 2 =

b 3 − 1 =   3 − 2 =   4 − 3 =   5 − 1 =

c 4 − 2 =   2 − 0 =   4 − 1 =   1 − 0 =

d 3 − 2 =   5 − 2 =   5 − 0 =   4 − 1 =

e 5 − 0 =   5 − 3 =   4 − 2 =   5 − 2 =

f 3 − 3 =   4 − 3 =   3 − 2 =   5 − 4 =

g 3 − 0 =   4 − 1 =   3 − 1 =   3 − 3 =

h 4 − 4 =   5 − 0 =   4 − 3 =   2 − 1 =

i 5 − 3 =   4 − 2 =   5 − 1 =   4 − 3 =

j 5 − 2 =   3 − 3 =   1 − 0 =   5 − 1 =

Mark   Time Taken

Test 7

Subtraction facts of numbers to 10

a   4 – 2 =   6 – 5 =   5 – 3 =   6 – 1 =

b   5 – 3 =   4 – 4 =   7 – 5 =   4 – 3 =

c   6 – 3 =   5 – 3 =   6 – 1 =   5 – 2 =

d   5 – 4 =   7 – 5 =   4 – 2 =   6 – 4 =

e   7 – 2 =   4 – 3 =   6 – 3 =   7 – 1 =

f   5 – 0 =   7 – 3 =   3 – 0 =   7 – 5 =

g   7 – 3 =   4 – 2 =   5 – 2 =   6 – 3 =

h   6 – 1 =   6 – 0 =   3 – 1 =   5 – 1 =

i   4 – 3 =   5 – 4 =   7 – 3 =   8 – 4 =

j   6 – 0 =   4 – 1 =   6 – 5 =   3 – 2 =

Mark   Time Taken

Test 8

Subtraction facts of numbers to 10

a $7 - 4 =$ $5 - 2 =$ $4 - 3 =$ $8 - 4 =$

b $8 - 5 =$ $7 - 4 =$ $5 - 4 =$ $7 - 5 =$

c $3 - 2 =$ $5 - 4 =$ $7 - 4 =$ $6 - 3 =$

d $7 - 2 =$ $5 - 2 =$ $6 - 3 =$ $7 - 1 =$

e $3 - 2 =$ $6 - 3 =$ $3 - 1 =$ $5 - 2 =$

f $5 - 4 =$ $7 - 2 =$ $8 - 4 =$ $4 - 3 =$

g $4 - 0 =$ $8 - 2 =$ $3 - 3 =$ $6 - 2 =$

h $6 - 3 =$ $3 - 2 =$ $7 - 3 =$ $3 - 1 =$

i $7 - 5 =$ $4 - 4 =$ $5 - 1 =$ $5 - 4 =$

j $5 - 3 =$ $6 - 2 =$ $7 - 5 =$ $6 - 0 =$

Mark

Time Taken

Test 9

Mixed addition and subtraction

a $0 + 3 =$ ▢ $2 + 4 =$ ▢ $2 + 7 =$ ▢ $0 + 4 =$ ▢

b $5 - 2 =$ ▢ $5 - 4 =$ ▢ $4 - 2 =$ ▢ $4 - 3 =$ ▢

c ▢ $+ 4 = 10$ ▢ $+ 1 = 10$ ▢ $+ 3 = 10$ ▢ $+ 6 = 10$

d $6 - 2 =$ ▢ $5 - 3 =$ ▢ $7 - 3 =$ ▢ $4 - 1 =$ ▢

e $10 +$ ▢ $= 10$ $9 +$ ▢ $= 10$ $5 +$ ▢ $= 10$ $1 +$ ▢ $= 10$

f $5 + 1 =$ ▢ $3 + 1 =$ ▢ $0 + 5 =$ ▢ $3 + 2 =$ ▢

g $6 - 5 =$ ▢ $4 - 0 =$ ▢ $3 - 2 =$ ▢ $5 - 3 =$ ▢

h $2 +$ ▢ $= 10$ $3 +$ ▢ $= 10$ $8 +$ ▢ $= 10$ $7 +$ ▢ $= 10$

i $4 - 3 =$ ▢ $7 - 0 =$ ▢ $6 - 4 =$ ▢ $5 - 3 =$ ▢

j $5 - 5 =$ ▢ $6 - 2 =$ ▢ $7 - 5 =$ ▢ $6 - 0 =$ ▢

Mark ▢   Time Taken ▢

15

Mixed addition and subtraction

a ☐ $+ 8 = 10$ ☐ $+ 1 = 10$ ☐ $+ 6 = 10$ ☐ $+ 4 = 10$

b $7 - 4 =$ ☐ $5 - 2 =$ ☐ $4 - 3 =$ ☐ $8 - 4 =$ ☐

c $3 + 3 =$ ☐ $1 + 2 =$ ☐ $2 +$ ☐ $= 10$ $4 +$ ☐ $= 10$

d $1 +$ ☐ $= 10$ $0 +$ ☐ $= 10$ $3 +$ ☐ $= 10$ $5 +$ ☐ $= 10$

e $7 - 2 =$ ☐ $5 - 2 =$ ☐ $6 - 3 =$ ☐ $7 - 1 =$ ☐

f $3 - 2 =$ ☐ $6 - 3 =$ ☐ $3 - 1 =$ ☐ $5 - 2 =$ ☐

g ☐ $+ 7 = 10$ ☐ $+ 5 = 10$ ☐ $+ 1 = 10$ ☐ $+ 8 = 10$

h $3 + 4 =$ ☐ $4 + 1 =$ ☐ $3 + 1 =$ ☐ $0 + 3 =$ ☐

i $5 - 4 =$ ☐ $7 - 2 =$ ☐ $8 - 5 =$ ☐ $4 - 3 =$ ☐

j $8 - 5 =$ ☐ $5 - 4 =$ ☐ $6 - 4 =$ ☐ $7 - 5 =$ ☐

Mark ☐   Time Taken ☐

Test 11

Mixed addition and subtraction

a $9 - 5 =$ $8 - 4 =$ $6 - 4 =$ $7 - 3 =$

b $5 + 2 =$ $4 + 1 =$ $5 + 3 =$ $2 + 5 =$

c $5 +$ $= 10$ $2 +$ $= 10$ $9 +$ $= 10$ $10 +$ $= 10$

d $3 + 1 =$ $5 + 2 =$ $4 + 2 =$ $4 + 6 =$

e $4 + 2 =$ $3 + 7 =$ $4 + 3 =$ $2 + 0 =$

f $4 - 2 =$ $6 - 4 =$ $5 - 4 =$ $8 - 3 =$

g $0 + 5 =$ $4 + 3 =$ $1 + 5 =$ $5 + 2 =$

h $7 - 4 =$ $5 - 2 =$ $4 - 3 =$ $8 - 4 =$

i $8 +$ $= 10$ $1 +$ $= 10$ $+ 1 = 10$ $+ 7 = 10$

j $+ 3 = 10$ $+ 8 = 10$ $+ 2 = 10$ $+ 5 = 10$

Mark   Time Taken

17

Word problems

a I have 2 cats and Jo has 4 cats.
How many cats do we have altogether?

b What is the sum of 5 and 4?

c How many more than 3 is 5?

d What number do I add to 3 to make 10?

e Simon has £2. He is given £8 more.
How much does he have now?

f Ben is 4 years older than Jo. Ben is 9.
How old is Jo?

g 9 people are on a bus. 7 people get off.
How many are on the bus now?

h I think of a number then I add 3. The answer is 7.
What is my number?

i Rob is 5 years older than Ella. Ella is 3.
How old is Rob?

j I think of a number then I subtract 6. The answer is 8.
What is my number?

Mark   Time Taken

Doubles of numbers

a) double 2 =   double 3 =   double 5 =   double 4 =

b) 5 x 2 =   6 x 2 =   3 x 2 =   4 x 2 =

c) 2 + 2 =   4 + 4 =   5 + 5 =   6 + 6 =

d) twice 6 =   twice 2 =   twice 4 =   twice 7 =

e) 7 x 2 =   1 x 2 =   0 x 2 =   8 x 2 =

f) double 7 =   double 4 =   double 8 =   double 6 =

g) 3 + 3 =   5 + 5 =   9 + 9 =   7 + 7 =

h) 6 + 6 =   9 + 9 =   10 + 10 =   8 + 8 =

i) twice 10 =   twice 8 =   twice 9 =   twice 11 =

j) 12 x 2 =   13 x 2 =   9 x 2 =   15 x 2 =

Mark   Time Taken

Doubles of numbers

a   double 1 =   double 5 =   double 0 =   double 3 =

b   7 x 2 =   2 x 2 =   3 x 2 =   5 x 2 =

c   3 + 3 =   6 + 6 =   5 + 5 =   8 + 8 =

d   twice 5 =   twice 9 =   twice 1 =   twice 7 =

e   8 x 2 =   5 x 2 =   7 x 2 =   6 x 2 =

f   double 6 =   double 9 =   double 10 =   double 4 =

g   0 + 0 =   15 + 15 =   9 + 9 =   8 + 8 =

h   11 + 11 =   9 + 9 =   12 + 12 =   7 + 7 =

i   twice 12 =   twice 7 =   twice 6 =   twice 13 =

j   14 x 2 =   12 x 2 =   11 x 2 =   13 x 2 =

Mark   Time Taken

Test 15

Count on and back in 2s, 5s, 10s

a   2, 4, 6, 8   5, 10, 15, 20   10, 20, 30, 40

b   10, 15, 20, 25   20, 30, 40, 50   4, 6, 8, 10

c   10, 8, 6, 4   40, 30, 20, 10   25, 20, 15, 10

d   15, 20, 25, 30   30, 40, 50, 60   6, 8, 10, 12

e   12, 10, 8, 6   50, 40, 30, 20   30, 25, 20, 15

f   20, 25, 30, 35   40, 50, 60, 70   8, 10, 12, 14

g   14, 12, 10, 8   60, 50, 40, 30   35, 30, 25, 20

h   25, 30, 35, 40   50, 60, 70, 80   10, 12, 14, 16

i   16, 14, 12, 10   70, 60, 50, 40   40, 35, 30, 25

j   30, 35, 40, 45   60, 70, 80, 90   12, 14, 16, 18

Mark   Time Taken

Count on and back in 2s, 5s, 10s

a 4, 6, 8, 10   10, 15, 20, 25   20, 30, 40, 50

b 20, 25, 30, 35   30, 40, 50, 60   6, 8, 10, 12

c 12, 10, 8, 6   35, 30, 25, 20   50, 40, 30, 20

d 25, 30, 35, 40   30, 40, 50, 60   10, 12, 14, 16

e 70, 60, 50, 40   16, 14, 12, 10   40, 35, 30, 25

f 30, 35, 40, 45   40, 50, 60, 70   8, 10, 12, 14

g 18, 16, 14, 12   45, 40, 35, 30   80, 70, 60, 50

h 35, 40, 45, 50   50, 60, 70, 80   12, 14, 16, 18

i 90, 80, 70, 60   20, 18, 16, 14   5, 10, 15, 20

j 40, 45, 50, 55   60, 70, 80, 90   16, 18, 20, 22

Mark   Time Taken

Mixed addition, subtraction, multiplication and counting on

a $0 + 3 =$ ⬜ $8 \times 2 =$ ⬜ $2 + 4 =$ ⬜ $0 + 4 =$ ⬜

b $7 \times 2 =$ ⬜ $5 - 4 =$ ⬜ 40, 35, 30 ⬜ $4 - 3 =$ ⬜

c ⬜ $+ 4 = 10$ ⬜ $+ 1 = 10$ twice 9 = ⬜ ⬜ $+ 6 = 10$

d 35, 40, 45 ⬜ 40, 50, 60 ⬜ $7 - 3 =$ ⬜ $4 - 1 =$ ⬜

e $10 +$ ⬜ $= 10$ $9 +$ ⬜ $= 10$ $5 +$ ⬜ $= 10$ 25, 30, 35 ⬜

f $3 + 3 =$ ⬜ $5 \times 2 =$ ⬜ $5 + 5 =$ ⬜ $8 + 8 =$ ⬜

g twice 5 = ⬜ ⬜ $+ 3 = 10$ twice 1 = ⬜ 80, 70, 60 ⬜

h $2 + 4 =$ ⬜ $6 + 6 =$ ⬜ $5 - 2 =$ ⬜ $6 \times 2 =$ ⬜

i $1 +$ ⬜ $= 10$ $5 - 3 =$ ⬜ 12, 14, 16 ⬜ $6 - 2 =$ ⬜

j 70, 60, 50 ⬜ 16, 14, 12 ⬜ $4 - 2 =$ ⬜ twice 7 = ⬜

Mark ⬜ Time Taken ⬜

Test 18

Mixed addition, subtraction, multiplication and counting on

a 18, 16, 14 ☐ ☐   ☐ + 1 = 10   ☐ + 6 = 10   ☐ + 4 = 10

b 7 − 4 = ☐   5 − 2 = ☐   40, 50, 60 ☐   8 − 4 = ☐

c 70, 60, 50 ☐   1 + 2 = ☐   40, 35, 30, 25 ☐   4 + ☐ = 10

d 1 + ☐ = 10   80, 70, 60 ☐   3 + ☐ = 10   5 + ☐ = 10

e 7 − 2 = ☐   double 4 = ☐   6 − 3 = ☐   7 − 1 = ☐

f double 7 = ☐   5 − 4 = ☐   double 8 = ☐   8 + 8 = ☐

g 3 + 3 = ☐   10, 12, 14 ☐   9 + 9 = ☐   7 + 7 = ☐

h double 6 = ☐   16, 14, 12 ☐   2 + ☐ = 10   35, 40, 45 ☐

i 30, 35, 40 ☐   4 − 3 = ☐   5 + 5 = ☐   6 + ☐ = 10

j ☐ + 8 = 10   45, 40, 35 ☐   0 + ☐ = 10   double 9 = ☐

Mark ☐   Time Taken ☐

Test 19

Mixed addition, subtraction, multiplication and counting on

a   35, 40, 45 ☐   3 + 1 = ☐   10, 12, 14 ☐   ☐ + 1 = 10

b   4 + 2 = ☐   80, 70, 60 ☐   6 − 4 = ☐   15 + 15 = ☐

c   3 + 1 = ☐   double 5 = ☐   4 + 2 = ☐   4 + 3 = ☐

d   18, 16, 14 ☐   twice 7 = ☐   twice 13 = ☐   2 + 0 = ☐

e   4 − 2 = ☐   45, 40, 35 ☐   5 − 4 = ☐   8 − 3 = ☐

f   5 + 2 = ☐   double 9 = ☐   ☐ + 2 = 10   double 4 = ☐

g   0 + 0 = ☐   ☐ + 5 = 10   9 + 9 = ☐   8 + 8 = ☐

h   8 + ☐ = 10   1 + ☐ = 10   40, 45, 50 ☐   ☐ + 7 = 10

i   ☐ + 3 = 10   ☐ + 8 = 10   double 10 = ☐   100, 90, 80 ☐

j   twice 11 = ☐   50, 60, 70 ☐   twice 6 = ☐   4 + 3 = ☐

Mark ☐   Time Taken ☐

25

Mixed addition, subtraction, multiplication and counting on

a   50, 40, 30 ☐   7 + 1 = ☐   18, 16, 14 ☐   ☐ + 7 = 10

b   6 + 2 = ☐   90, 80, 70 ☐   9 − 5 = ☐   ☐ + 6 = 10

c   3 + 2 = ☐   14 + 14 = ☐   9 − 1 = ☐   5 + 3 = ☐

d   20, 18, 16 ☐   twice 8 = ☐   twice 12 = ☐   8 + 0 = ☐

e   4 − 4 = ☐   50, 45, 40 ☐   8 − 4 = ☐   4 + 4 = ☐

f   double 6 = ☐   ☐ + 3 = 10   ☐ + 6 = 10   double 4 = ☐

g   0 + 7 = ☐   6 + 2 = ☐   9 + 9 = ☐   7 + 7 = ☐

h   7 + ☐ = 10   4 + ☐ = 10   45, 50, 55 ☐   ☐ + 4 = 10

i   double 11 = ☐   ☐ + 2 = 10   double 12 = ☐   90, 80, 70 ☐

j   twice 10 = ☐   60, 70, 80 ☐   twice 6 = ☐   4 + 5 = ☐

Mark ☐   Time Taken ☐

Test 21

Word problems

a What is the total of 5 and 4?

b How many less than 12 is 5?

c What number do I subtract from 13 to make 6?

d Sam has £13. He spends £8.
How much does he have left?

e It is 10 o'clock. I got up 3 hours ago.
What time did I get up?

f 6 people are wearing hats. Twice as many are not wearing hats.
How many are not wearing hats?

g I think of a number then I double it. The answer is 16.
What is my number?

h What number comes next: 14, 12, 10, ...?

i What number is double 11?

j Paul buys a ball for £9. Jill buys a ball that costs twice as much.
How much did Jill's ball cost?

Mark   Time Taken

27

Answers

Test 1

a	5	5	4	2
b	3	6	4	2
c	4	8	4	3
d	4	3	4	5
e	6	6	8	5
f	5	5	6	3
g	6	4	5	8
h	5	5	4	7
i	4	4	5	4
j	4	4	3	6

Test 3

a	1	0	5	7
b	3	4	8	5
c	2	9	1	6
d	0	3	7	4
e	9	6	0	3
f	1	0	7	8
g	2	8	1	6
h	9	5	8	2
i	4	1	2	7
j	9	2	6	5

Test 2

a	5	7	4	3
b	5	7	3	4
c	5	5	5	4
d	7	3	4	5
e	4	4	5	6
f	6	6	2	3
g	6	4	6	3
h	6	8	6	6
i	4	5	8	6
j	6	3	5	8

Test 4

a	0	7	1	3
b	1	8	7	2
c	7	6	4	8
d	4	0	2	9
e	8	4	6	5
f	4	5	7	8
g	2	10	4	1
h	0	1	6	10
i	5	0	3	7
j	8	6	1	9

Test 5

a	0	1	1	3
b	1	1	2	2
c	4	5	0	0
d	3	2	2	1
e	0	2	4	2
f	2	1	4	3
g	3	2	1	2
h	4	1	0	1
i	3	1	0	1
j	3	2	2	1

Test 6

a	3	1	2	1
b	2	1	1	4
c	2	2	3	1
d	1	3	5	3
e	5	2	2	3
f	0	1	1	1
g	3	3	2	0
h	0	5	1	1
i	2	2	4	1
j	3	0	1	4

Test 7

a	2	1	2	5
b	2	0	2	1
c	3	2	5	3
d	1	2	2	2
e	5	1	3	6
f	5	4	3	2
g	4	2	3	3
h	5	6	2	4
i	1	1	4	4
j	6	3	1	1

Test 8

a	3	3	1	4
b	3	3	1	2
c	1	1	3	3
d	5	3	3	6
e	1	3	2	3
f	1	5	4	1
g	4	6	0	4
h	3	1	4	2
i	2	0	4	1
j	2	4	2	6

Test 9

a	3	6	9	4
b	3	1	2	1
c	6	9	7	4
d	4	2	4	3
e	0	1	5	9
f	6	4	5	5
g	1	4	1	2
h	8	7	2	3
i	1	7	2	2
j	0	4	2	6

Test 11

a	4	4	2	4
b	7	5	8	7
c	5	8	1	0
d	4	7	6	10
e	6	10	7	2
f	2	2	1	5
g	5	7	6	7
h	3	3	1	4
i	2	9	9	3
j	7	2	8	5

Test 10

a	2	9	4	6
b	3	3	1	4
c	6	3	8	6
d	9	10	7	5
e	5	3	3	6
f	1	3	2	3
g	3	5	9	2
h	7	5	4	3
i	1	5	3	1
j	3	1	2	2

Test 12

a	6
b	9
c	2
d	7
e	£10
f	5
g	2
h	4
i	8
j	14

Test 13

a	4	6	10	8
b	10	12	6	8
c	4	8	10	12
d	12	4	8	14
e	14	2	0	16
f	14	8	16	12
g	6	10	18	14
h	12	18	20	16
i	20	16	18	22
j	24	26	18	30

Test 15

a	10	25	50
b	30	60	12
c	2	0	5
d	35	70	14
e	4	10	10
f	40	80	16
g	6	20	15
h	45	90	18
i	8	30	20
j	50	100	20

Test 14

a	2	10	0	6
b	14	4	6	10
c	6	12	10	16
d	10	18	2	14
e	16	10	14	12
f	12	18	20	8
g	0	30	18	16
h	22	18	24	14
i	24	14	12	26
j	28	24	22	26

Test 16

a	12	30	60
b	40	70	14
c	4	15	10
d	45	70	18
e	30	8	20
f	50	80	16
g	10	25	40
h	55	90	20
i	50	12	25
j	60	100	24

Test 17

a	3	16	6	4
b	14	1	25	1
c	6	9	18	4
d	50	70	4	3
e	0	1	5	40
f	6	10	10	16
g	10	7	2	50
h	6	12	3	12
i	9	2	18	4
j	40	10	2	14

Test 18

a	12	9	4	6
b	3	3	70	4
c	40	3	20	6
d	9	50	7	5
e	5	8	3	6
f	14	1	16	16
g	6	16	18	14
h	12	10	8	50
i	45	1	10	4
j	2	30	10	18

Test 19

a	50	4	16	9
b	6	50	2	30
c	4	10	6	7
d	12	14	26	2
e	2	30	1	5
f	7	18	8	8
g	0	5	18	16
h	2	9	55	3
i	7	2	20	70
j	22	80	12	7

Test 20

a	20	8	12	3
b	8	60	4	4
c	5	28	8	8
d	14	16	24	8
e	0	35	4	8
f	12	7	4	8
g	7	8	18	14
h	3	6	60	6
i	22	8	24	60
j	20	90	12	9

Test 21

a	9
b	7
c	7
d	£5
e	7 o'clock
f	12
g	8
h	8
i	22
j	£18